MY OWN SEASONS

Twenty Four Illustrated Poems

Brigit Byron Coons

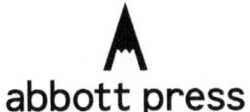
abbott press

Abbott Press books may be ordered through booksellers or by contacting:

Abbott Press
1663 Liberty Drive
Bloomington, IN 47403
www.abbottpress.com
Phone: 1 (866) 697-5310

Because of the dynamic nature of the Internet, any web addresses or links contained in this book may have changed since publication and may no longer be valid. The views expressed in this work are solely those of the author and do not necessarily reflect the views of the publisher, and the publisher hereby disclaims any responsibility for them.

ISBN: 978-1-4582-2007-3 (sc)
ISBN: 978-1-4582-2008-0 (e)

Library of Congress Control Number: 2016904175

Print information available on the last page.

Abbott Press rev. date: 10/13/2016

This cherished collection of poems I proudly
dedicate to my beloved friend,

Paige

Who was still sitting in a folding chair at our
support group when I returned,
twelve years later; with sad smiles and happy tears.

Contents

Acknowledgements

I want to express my sincere gratitude to all who have helped me create this collection of verse. To the many people who have voiced their support and enthusiasm as I read portions of the work to them over dinners and dates and deliriums of days in the making; I thank you.

Also, to Abbott Press and the crew, whom I have worked with over the many months in preparation for the publication and joyous release of <u>My Own Seasons</u>; I thank you.

And to my friends and family that have encouraged my efforts, all of whom have ignited my passion to share my writing with all who will listen: Kismet, River, Madeline, Klaus, Annie, Paige, Claire, Cricket, Melisa, Irene, Aileen, Pat, Julie, Paulette, and last but not least, my two dear cats; Willow and Phoenicia; I thank you.

Special thanks go to all the wonderful and interesting people that have enriched my life's experience beyond measure at the Billy DeFrank LGBTQ Silicon Valley Community Center in San Jose California. You have been there for me through my darkest nights and brightest days of my journey back to sanity and pride.

Lastly, with gratitude beyond mortal measure, from deep in my soul, I thank my spiritual community at UNITY Palo Alto. You are my light, my guidance, my hope, my dreams, my love; forever.

And to you my unknown reader for acknowledging my prattling poems others ignore;

I thank you.

Brigit Byron Coons

List of Illustrations

The illustrations for these poems, with a few exceptions, were originally created by the author in color.

To view: www.myownseasons.brigit-byron-coons.com

Poem: **Brigitte**
Illustration Title: <u>Inner Beauty of Outer Space</u>
Dimensions: 30in. x 40in.
Medium: Acrylic on gesso primed illustration board.

Poem: **Do You Know What It Is Like?**
Illustration Title: <u>Something About Selena</u>
Dimensions: 18in. x 24in.
Medium: Acrylic on gesso primed illustration board.

Poem: **Divas Door**
Illustration Title: <u>FUN AT PARTIES</u>
Dimensions: 30in. x 40in.
Medium: Acrylic on gesso primed illustration board.

Poem: **ELIXER**
Illustration Title: <u>Typhoon</u>
Dimensions: 14in. x 24in.
Medium: Acrylic on gesso primed illustration board.

Poem: **For All the Right Reasons**
Illustration Title: <u>Story Time vol.1</u>
Dimensions: 19in. x 30in.
Medium: Acrylic on gesso primed illustration board.

Poem: **Permission Granted**
Illustration Title: <u>Little Treasure</u>
Dimensions: 20in. x 30in.
Medium: Acrylic on gesso primed illustration board.

Poem: **Let Go**
Illustration Title: <u>Timeless</u>
Dimensions: 30in. x 40in.
Medium: Acrylic on gesso primed illustration board.

Poem: **My Own Seasons**
Illustration Title: <u>Equation of Time</u>
Dimensions: 4ft. x 5ft. x 3in.
Medium: Acrylic on gesso primed wrapped canvas.

Poem: **Polar Bears**
Illustration Title: <u>Captain Byron N. Coons, USAF</u>
Dimensions: 18in. x 24in.
Medium: Oil on gesso primed canvas.

Poem: **My Aunt Virginia**
Illustration Title: <u>Hour Glass</u>
Dimensions: 36in. x 48in.
Medium: Acrylic on gesso primed canvas.

Poem: **I Have Become**
Illustration Title: <u>Beauty of The Galaxies</u>
Dimensions: 20in. x 30in.
Medium: Acrylic on gesso primed illustration board.

Poem: **To Wear a Garden**
Illustration Title: <u>Sands of Time</u>
Dimensions: 40in. x 60in.
Medium: Acrylic on gesso primed canvas.

Poem: **Run Away Girl**
Illustration Title: Kismet
Dimensions: 24in. x 20in.
Medium: Acrylic on gesso primed illustration board.

Poem: **The Thaw**
Illustration Title: PACIFICA
Dimensions: 30in. x 40in.
Medium: Acrylic on gesso primed illustration board.

Poem: **Taryn Taryn**
Illustration Title: October Eve
Dimensions: 20in. x 30in.
Medium: Acrylic on gesso primed illustration board.

Poem: **Sings Like a Song**
Illustration Title: Nebula
Dimensions: 30in. x 40in.
Medium: Acrylic on gesso primed illustration board.

Poem: **Trans Atlantic**
Illustration Title: Time, catalyst of change
Dimensions: 36in. x 48in.
Medium: Oil on gesso primed canvas.

Poem: **Fame Game**
Illustration Title: Passage of Time
Dimensions: 15in. x 20in.
Medium: Acrylic on gesso primed illustration board.

Poem: **Moon Over The Mission**
Illustration Title: Story Time vol.2
Dimensions: 19in. x 30in.
Medium: Acrylic on gesso primed illustration board.

Poem: **WOW**
Illustration Title: <u>Green Spot</u>
Dimensions: 30in. x 40in.
Medium: Acrylic on gesso primed illustration board.

Poem: **#newGirl**
Illustration Title: <u>Stunner</u>
Dimensions: 10in. x 24in.
Medium: Acrylic on gesso primed illustration board.

Poem: **Beauty Bare**
Illustration Title: <u>Cabinet of Dreams</u>
Dimensions: 18in. x 24in.
Medium: Acrylic on gesso primed illustration board.

Poem: **Millennia**
Illustration Title: <u>Sundial of Antiquity</u>
Dimensions: 30in. x 40in.
Medium: Acrylic on gesso primed canvas.

Poem: **I Was the Bookworm**
Illustration Title: <u>Brigit Byron Coons 2012</u>
Dimensions: *width:*1200px height: 1336px
Medium: Camera and Photoshop
Photo: Josephine Brak
Production: Digital enhancement by permission - Brigit Byron Coons

Brigitte

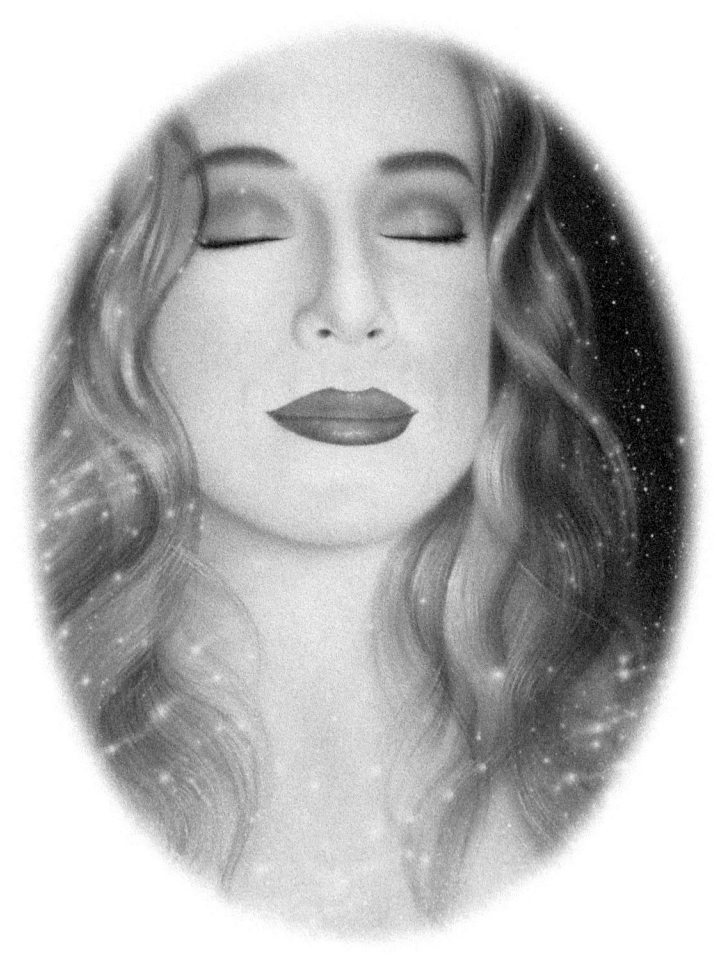

She sleeps restlessly,

in the Indigo moonlight,

of my hesitant soul.

Awaken now...

Do You Know
What It Is Like?

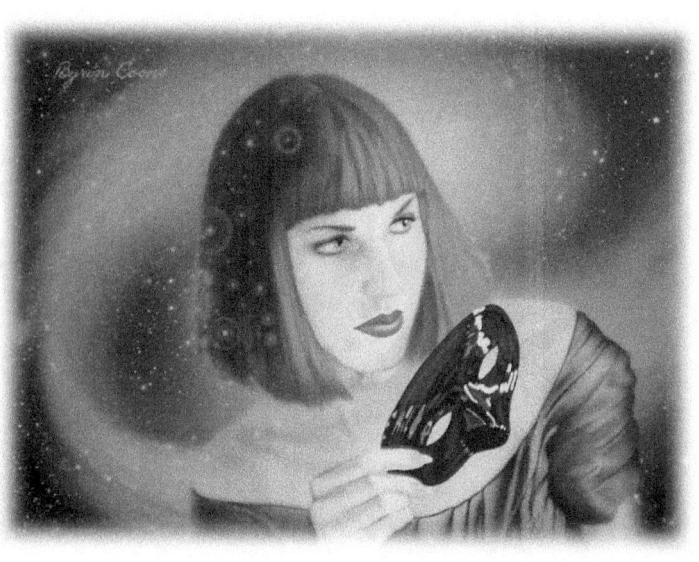

To hide inside as you are growing up,
even with all the people you know and talk with,
all the friends you play with and the ones you don't,
always holding back the truth even from yourself at times.

Do you know what is it like to hide you are a girl inside?
I do.

Always feeling her when you walk or awkwardly throw a ball,
or talk excitedly about something other than sports,
only to abruptly end the conversation.

Do you know what that is like?
I do.

Then to secretly hear them say, "Oh... he's just quiet, reads a lot, but;
kinda of weird.
Ya know?"

Do you know what it is like to hear that over and over about yourself?
I do.

And to be thinking all the while, **maybe** there will be a time
I will stand up,
look my parents in the eyes and say, "I am transgender,
I am a girl inside.
I need to come out now.
Will you still love me?"

This is my **maybe**...
I stand;
I look them all in the eyes and say, "I am transgender,
I am a girl inside.
I am coming out now.
Whatever you think of me;

I forgive you."

Divas Door

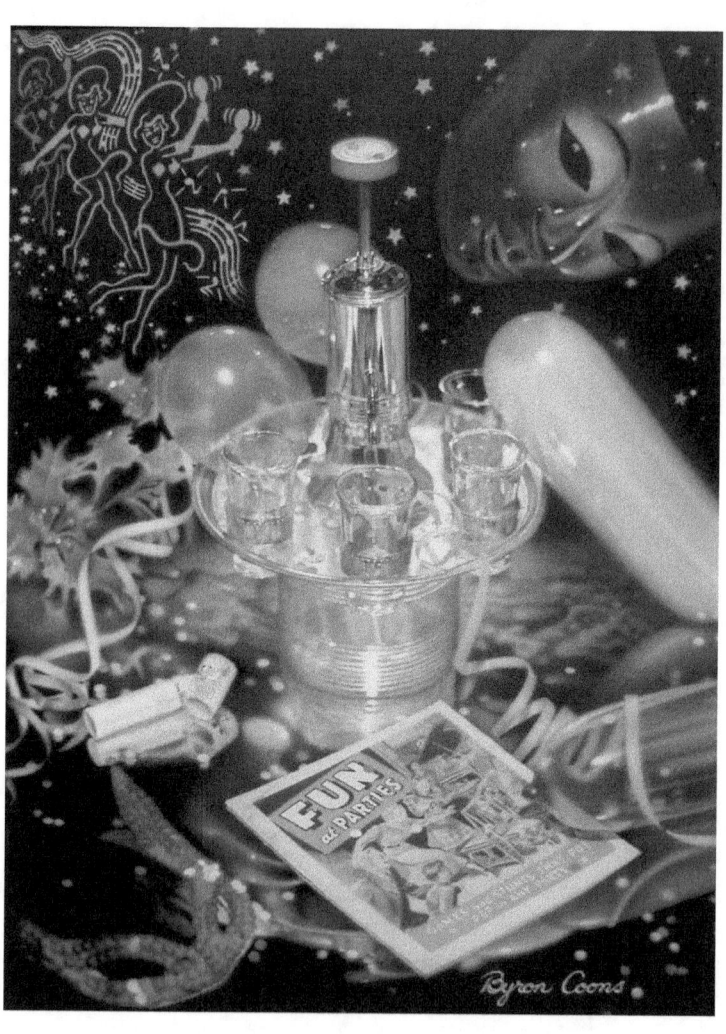

Byron Coons

We came up from the provincial badlands of the peninsula,
draped in our innocence and drag queen accessories;
to find our lost way to Divas door.

Innocents we were at the entrance of the decadents.

"Ladies free till eleven," she says with a smile I return;
while handing her my fare with anxious anticipation.

We are all boys here.
But who would know our secret,
and who would care.

But we care.
We are beautiful; and,
walk on as if we own it.

Once inside the dank elevator,
we ascend slowly to the dance floor,
smiling with happy girlish excitement.
Adjusting my twisted black bra strap;
side-straightening my short hem;
clearing my throat in falsetto;
and we are ready-to-rock.

Doors open and doors close behind us to reveal dimly lit rooms,
with bright colored musty walls reflecting phony disco effects,
off large vertical marbled mirrors towering to the ceiling.

Seamlessly we find ourselves in an underworld above The City.

Divas[1]
My heart races as I casually sit ass first,
with over-confident feminine grace,
high on a stiletto legged stool,
around a square wet bar,
enclosing a round dry girl;
we sit hiding our secret lusts,
taking it all in stride.

---

[1] Divas San Francisco's premier transgender nightclub.

Divas Door *continued*

We dance to a calliope of canned commercial cuts,
never caring if any of this is real.
Except, us; we are real.

In the fantasy of flight I have never felt so free,
in the motion and the magic of the music;
in the freeing of my gallant girl inside;
Out!

With arched back I sensually swing my skirted hips,
to long dated pop hits; in rhythmic expressions,
to the drum of my imaginary sexual desires,
loving every sinuous-pounding-beat,
of this pseudo primordial play.

I look around...
girls in black,
girls in red,
girls in love,
with themselves.

We can't help it.
Who else could love us?
We are the dammed,
while simultaneously:
the transgender blessed.

We dance,
we laugh,
we sweat,
then melt like flaming candlesticks,
into the dark desperate night.

ELIXIR

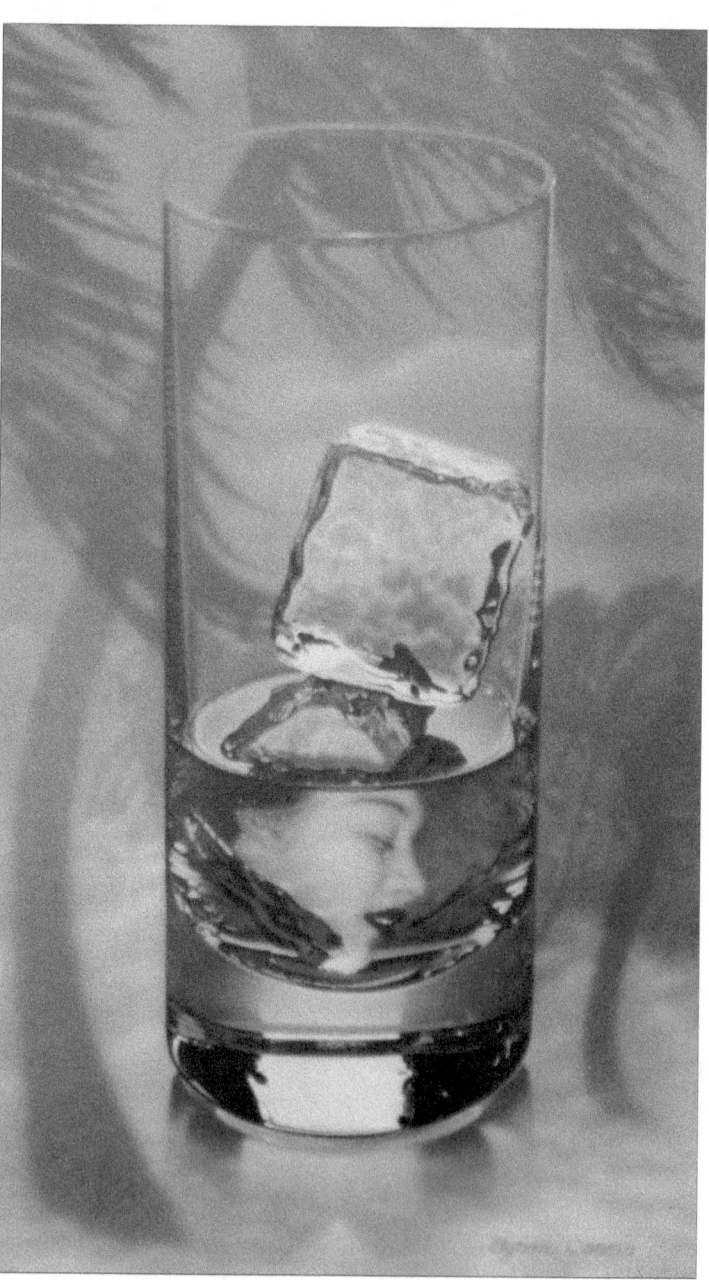

She turns to me with all seriousness and says, "Someday they will have a cure for this problem."

With this nervous belief could we have differed any further in our perceptions of transgender?

Someday? I will just take a pill? And the panacea of panaceas will cure this neurosis?

Is my desire to live as female just a fluke of my over-sexed imagination?

Could a new wonder drug reverse my compulsion to wear a skirt?

Is this just a cruel game my mind is playing on my weak soul?

Are all my responses to the world around me false?

Sadly, I know not.

She and I;

are doomed.

For All the Right
Reasons

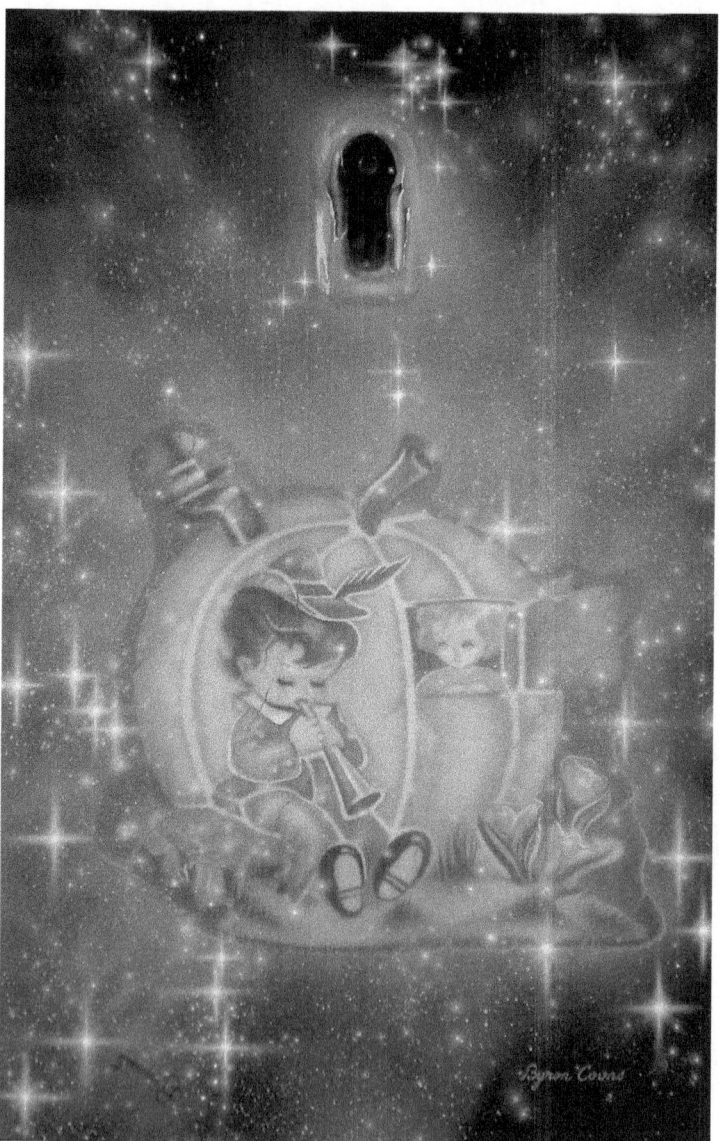

This time I am changing my life: completely.

Male to Female.

No turning back.

Inside; out.

Moving forward for all the right reasons.

The beautiful girl that lives inside me,

can no longer hide her truth.

I am coming out; now.

I face the street and brave the crowd with confident glisten.

I flip my soft blonde hair with attractive long-nail feminine grace.

To anyone who will hear my promise, "I am a happy T-girl."

I draw my eyeliner perfectly penciled deep above my long lashes,

like arched black wings that lift me into the starry night.

I wear the cloths I only dreamed to wear,

the way I dreamed to wear them,

countless secrets revealed.

For all the right reasons,

long at last,

I am,

free.

Permission Granted

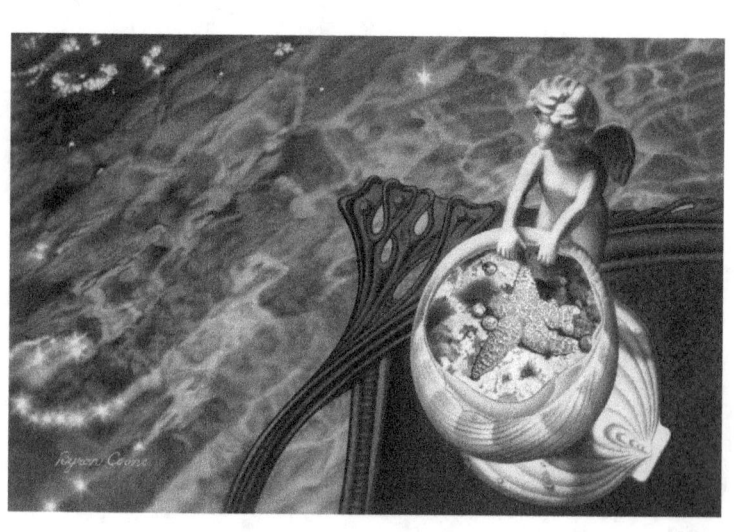

I give myself permission to realize my life long desire,
of prosperous, international recognition and success,
and celebrate my beloved gift of painting pictures,
to be shared with people all over the world.

I give myself permission to wear whatever I want to wear,
all day,
all night;
however I want to wear it.

I give myself permission to rest and dream,
imagining colors beyond RGB converted to CMYK,
in configurations of indeterminable resolution;
majestic visions with infinite spiraling potential.

I give myself permission to live however I want to live.
To have antiques and a vanity surrounded by old books,
nostalgia hung perfectly on the walls of my home,
with warm light and fresh air all around me.

I give myself permission...to be alive.

Let Go

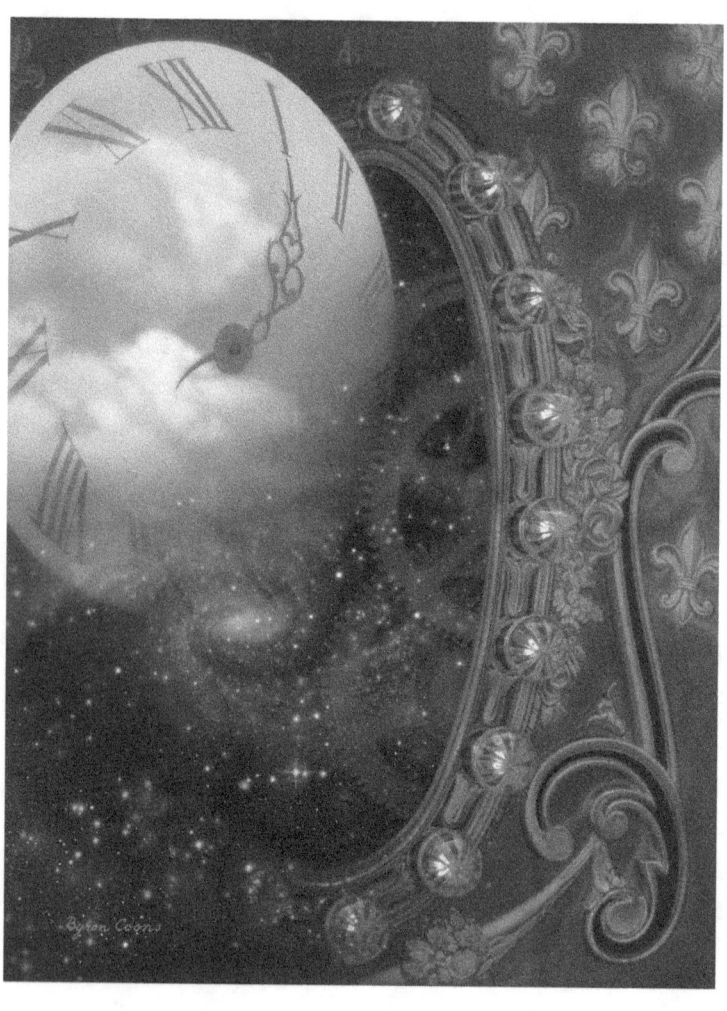

All those secret years
frozen in fear; falling
tears silently hidden.

Time to let it go.

You were just slowly finding your way
searching the deep darkness; lost
in the reticence of your soul.

Just let it all go.

For what divine luck
to have found what I was looking for, hidden
as Dorothy[2] said, "Right in my own backyard."

Let it go.

Be the girl you found latently waiting
inside your boyish shell: veiled.
Come out into the world;

Lovingly
Happily
Fully

(whispered softly)
Let go

---

[2] Dorothy the main character in L. Frank Baum's beloved classic story Wizard of Oz.

My Own Seasons

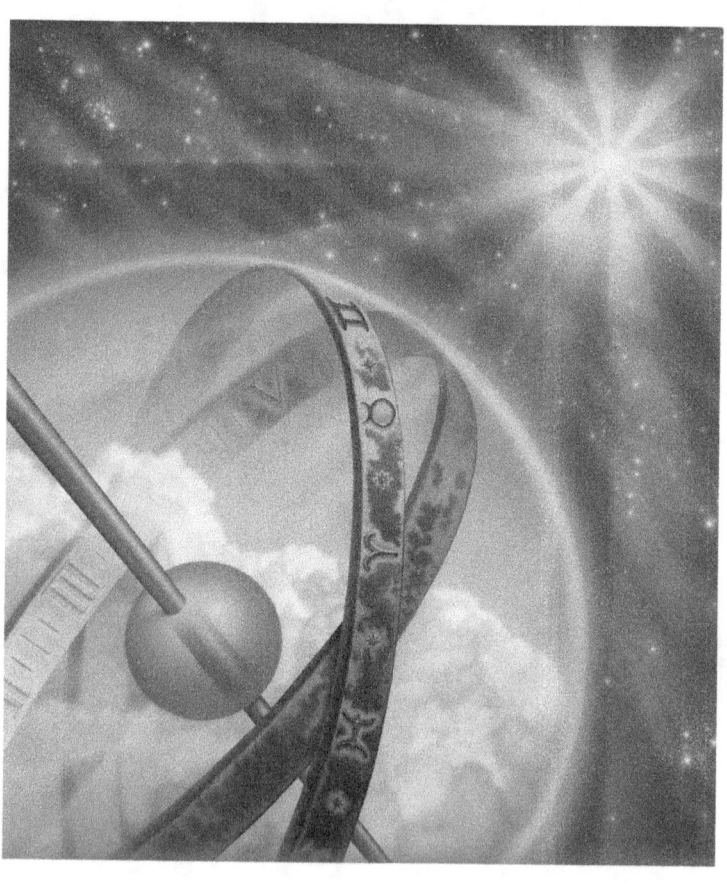

I have my own seasons,

my own storms to survive,

my own spring to celebrate;

the beauty of my epicene soul.

I have my own revolution to battle,

my own golden manifesto to proclaim,

my own position from which to express;

the heartfelt truth of my shaded gender.

I have my own stories to share,

my own errant legend to live,

even if no one is listening;

my own seasons change.

Polar Bears

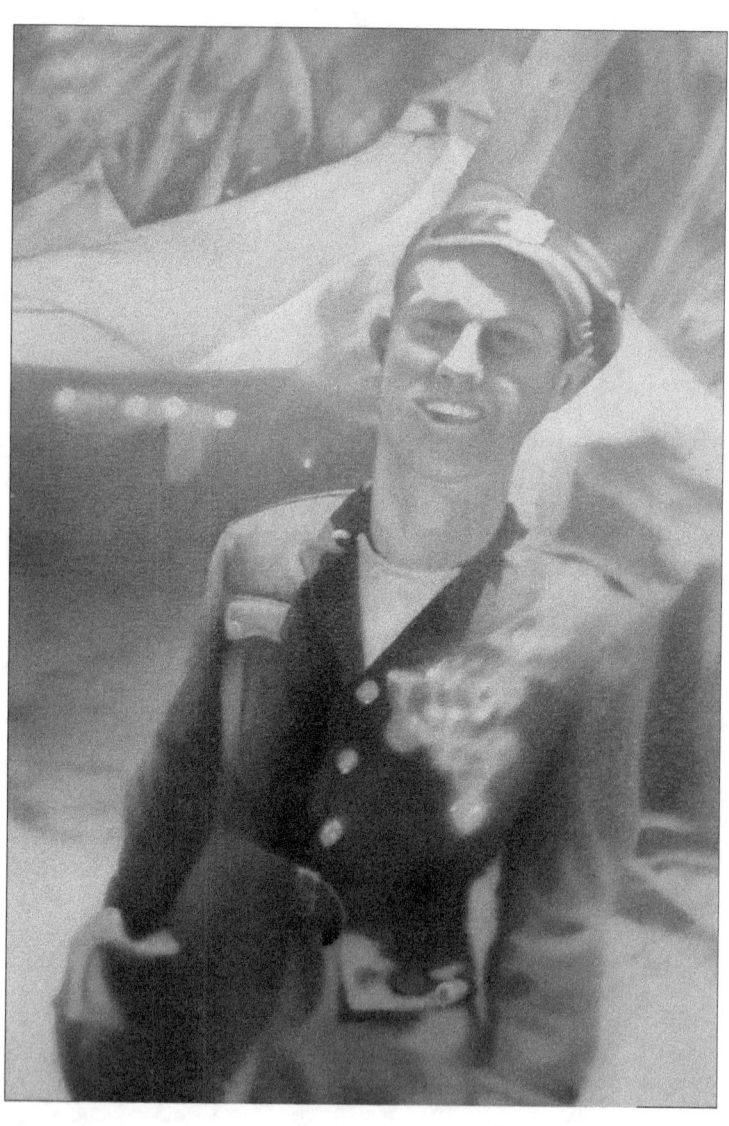

Captain Byron N. Coons, USAF

Beautiful boy
pretty girl
back-and-forth
in daily deliriums and dilemmas
of confused gender identity.

Handsome man
attractive woman
up-and-down we go
a steep stairway spiraling skyward
to archetypes illusionary and unattainable.

Sexy queen posed on the street
whore amongst the masses
queer to all who look
fallen freak to all
who turn away.

Like polar bears in a zoo we are
tepidly observed from afar
sub-obliquely evaluated
we walk our silly steps
sing our sad songs.

Surely they know we are
just men in messy make-up
just guys in blouses and bows
just high-heeled boys out to play.

I truly wish this were all that simple.

My Aunt Virginia

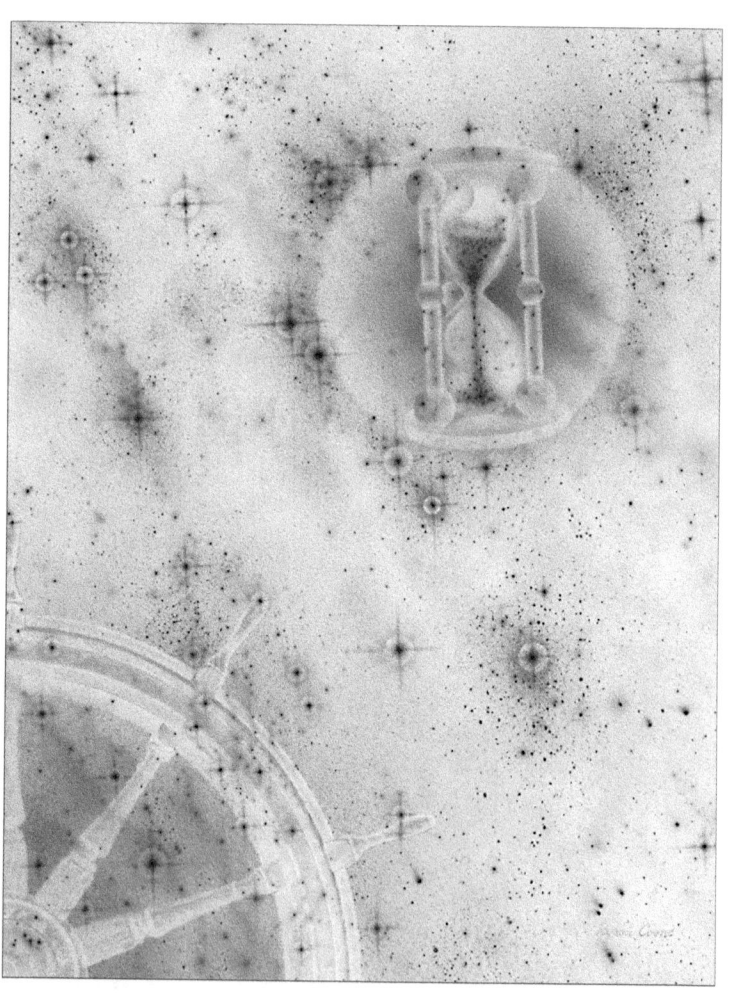

I loved my aunt.
And she loved me.
I was her favorite nephew,
of all my cousins,
or so she made me feel.

I wanted to look and be just like her many times.
Brown almond eyes always made-up perfectly.
Long manicured nails natural and polished.
Olive skin clear as the summer night sky.

When she spoke the room of chattering relatives would stop;
turn and listen, wide eyed waiting for her warm smile.

Her voice was friendly and low,
each word well thought through,
intelligent and relevant to the moment.

She loved the Arts and always encouraged my painting.
She was and still is my favorite aunt;

My Aunt Virginia

I Have Become

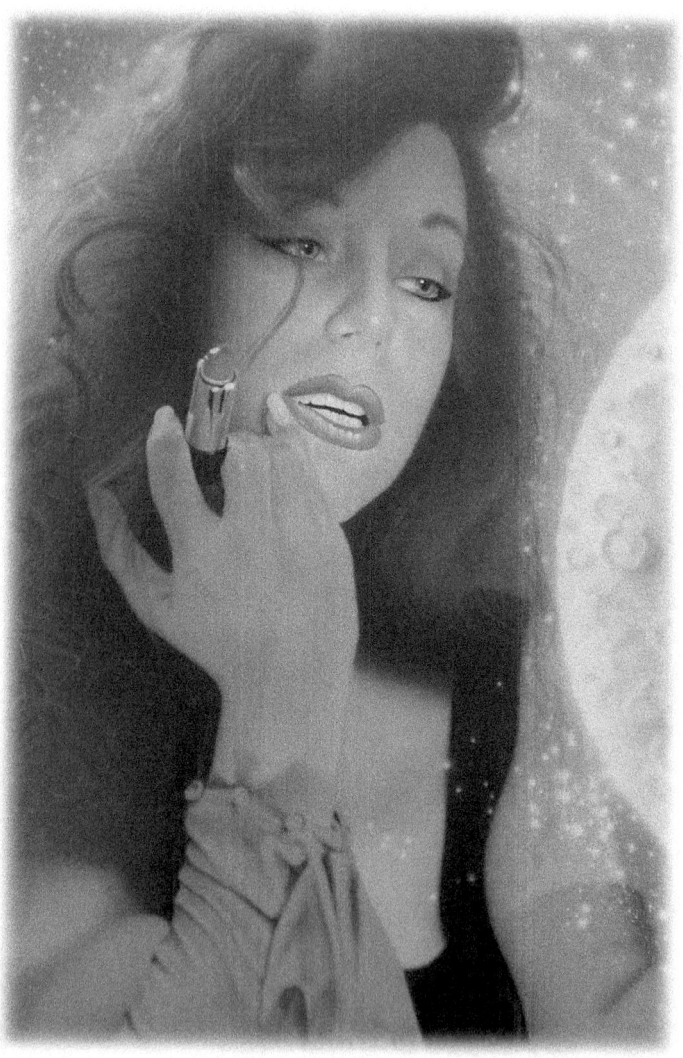

Like those pretty shop girls that work the vintage stores
along the Haight,
with wing shaped brows that arch high and way back;
Like only an artist could do.

With jet black eyeliner sharply countering the wing,
to sex appeal and attraction;
I submit.

Quietly enjoying the feminine inside my skinny shell,
I have become my girl inside out.
I have become;

Brigit

To Wear a Garden

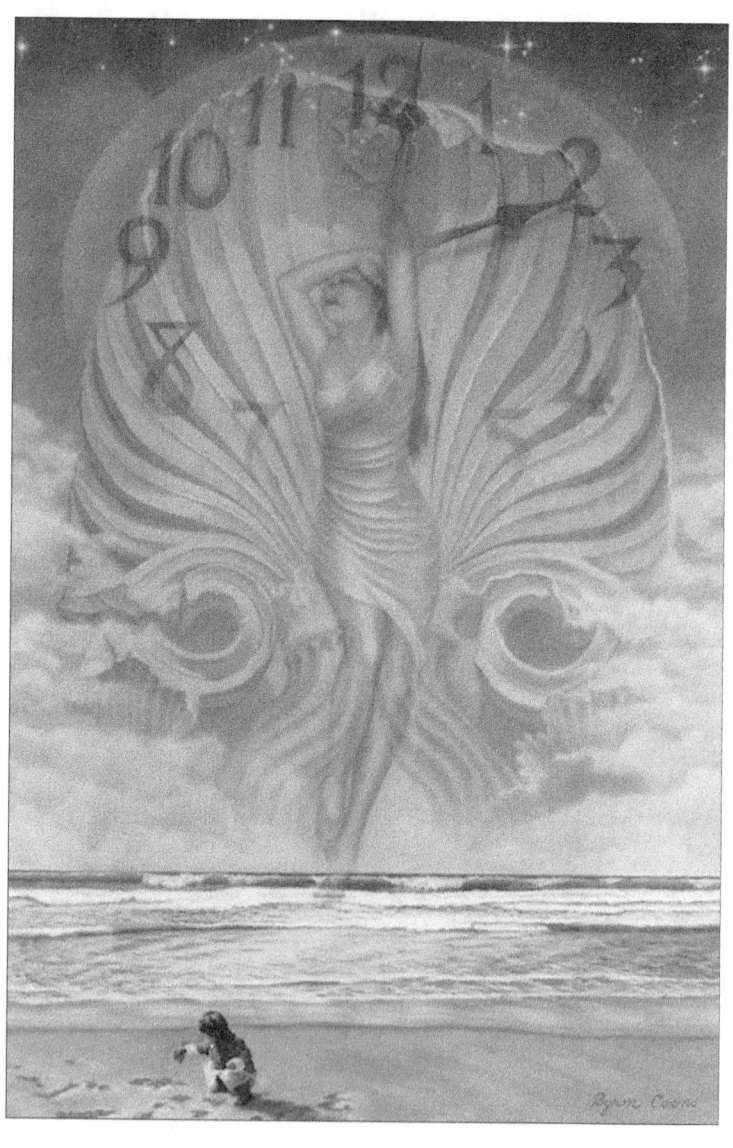

Ryan Coons

Cowboys and Indians
Quarterbacks to Captains
Policemen vested Presidents
redundant tailored themes
I can't wear anymore.

I prefer to wear a garden
robed in flush floral fantasy
brown spotted leopard lurking
under leafy patterns green
of sunrises and sonatas
colors magnificent
and matched.

In black boots and belts of belligerence
red round caps of your favorite team
I refuse to wear the accessories
of faded blue jean allegiance
to utilitarian schemes.

I prefer to quietly walk a gallery
silent images aquatic and deep
forms and space revolving
concepts clear and true.

Beards, burps and BO
boobs, butts and beers
your conversations bore me
your intensions simple and sad.

I prefer soft sunsets
atypical pictorial poems
colors scumbled imperfectly
across perfectly painted plains.

Excuse me from the huddle
need to change my shoes
then sense the world
around me and live
life as I choose.

Run Away Girl

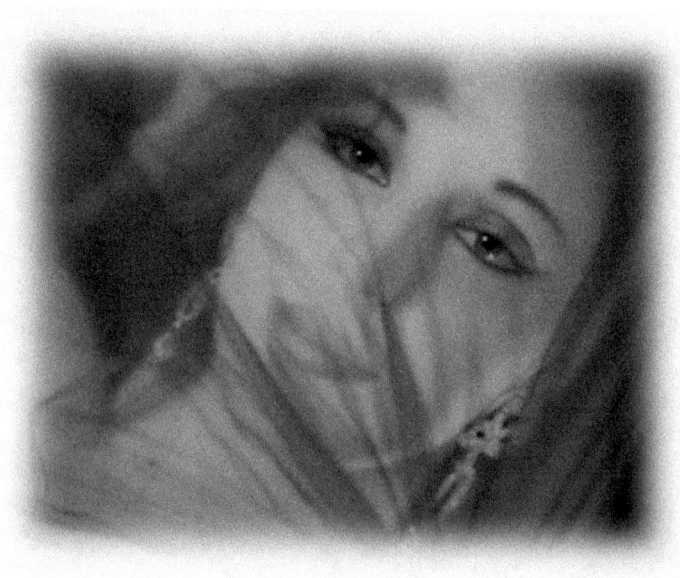

"I hate you."

"How could you be so selfish?"

"Get out of here."

"Just leave."

"No one wants you here anyway."

Your cruel words will echo empty in my fallen heart,

like cold raindrops on a dreaded rainy Monday;

for an eternity of sorrows.

Run away;

Hide away,

in the dark oblivion of futile self-denial.

Exploding inside with anguish; unfathomable,

love lost in black hot tears no one sees.

Your beloved sunny smile; gone;

forever.

Run away girl.

The Thaw

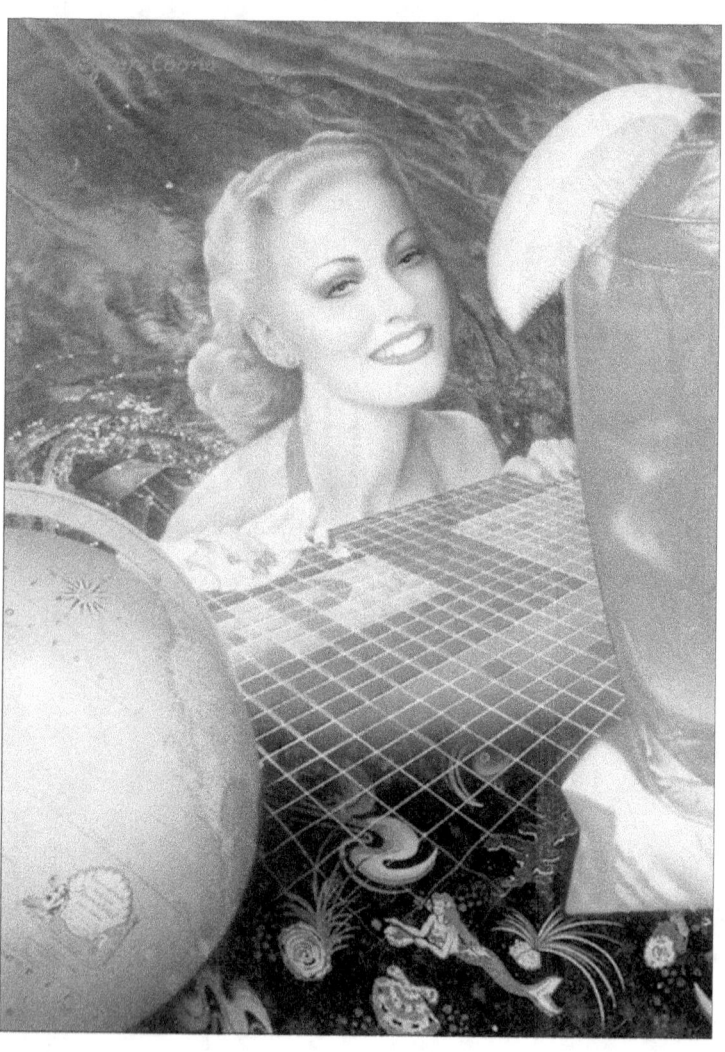

I have been dying in a deep freeze for twelve-cold-years.
You know the kind of unit?
Floor model, six feet long, rounded corners, opens from the top,
white, coffin-like heavy; self-imposed.

Yeah.

I lay there
motionless
silently screaming
inclined and forgotten like a frozen plastic bag of meat
encased in an icy suburban slab of conventions and conditions.

The thaw...

As I waited for the slow sun to melt my sea loose,
I discovered one of my arms to be not too stiff.
I gathered all the strength I have ever known,
reached out... and pushed... the switch... OFF.

Now I am thawing out like The Thing[3] under an electric blanket.
Time will surprise the camp with the transgender monster escaped,
it will send them running to their comfort zones of knitting normalcy.

I walk away from that deep freeze,
self-defrosted;

Warm again.

---

[3] The Thing from Another World (often referred to as The Thing) 1951 American
black-and-white science fiction/horror film produced by Howard Hawks.
Winchester Pictures Corporation, released by RKO Pictures.

Taryn Taryn

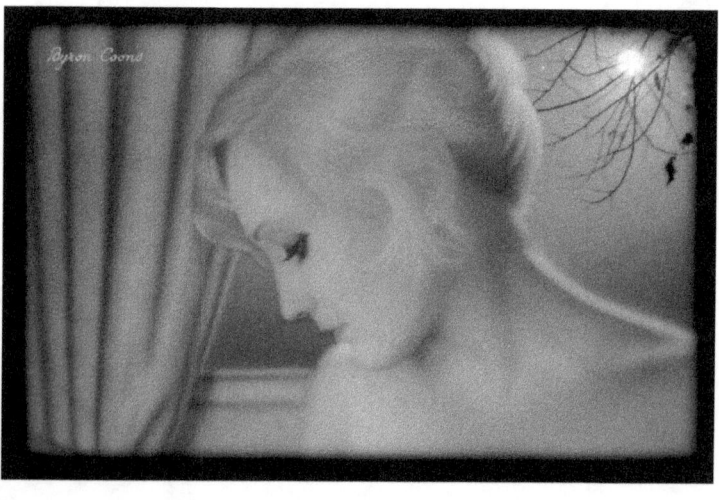

Hazel daisy lazy eyes,

luscious lips mouth,

blonde floppy mop,

tooth pick frame,

black sexy cloths.

You might have been the sister,

I painfully admired; instead,

you are a cherished friend,

I adore.

Let's go dancing tonight,

in the sparkling city.

Just us girls,

and burn;

The Floor.

Sings Like a Song

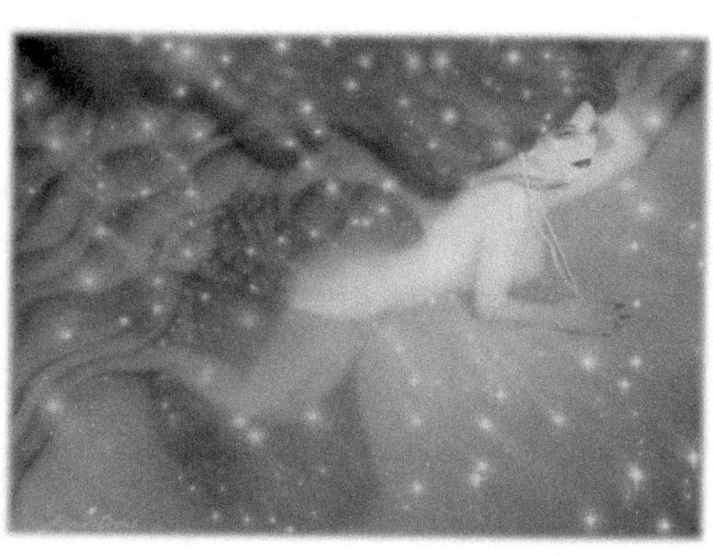

Sometimes it is all a little scary,
crossing the sea to my femininity;
like a green and golden pilgrimage,
to the Island of Cythera[4].

Other times it is all so wonderful,
quietly weeping with pure joy;
of my sentient self-discovery.

Always feeling my shape to be... female,
I shop the Haight in vintage style;
in graceful high-heeled stride.

I take it all so casually,
as I dress in black blouse and skirt;
loving every minute and every phony flirt.

I can't stop either Twyla Jane[5],
as I play your lonely video in cyberspace;
to synthesized feminine sensuality; that,

sings like a song.

---

[4] Island of Cythera, In Antiquity, Cythera, one of the Greek islands, was thought to have a serious claim to be the birthplace of Aphrodite, goddess of love. The island thus became sacred to Aphrodite and love.
[5] Twyla Jane / Twyla Jane Merzin, YouTube muse. Composer, actor and producer of incredible videos and animation.

Trans Atlantic

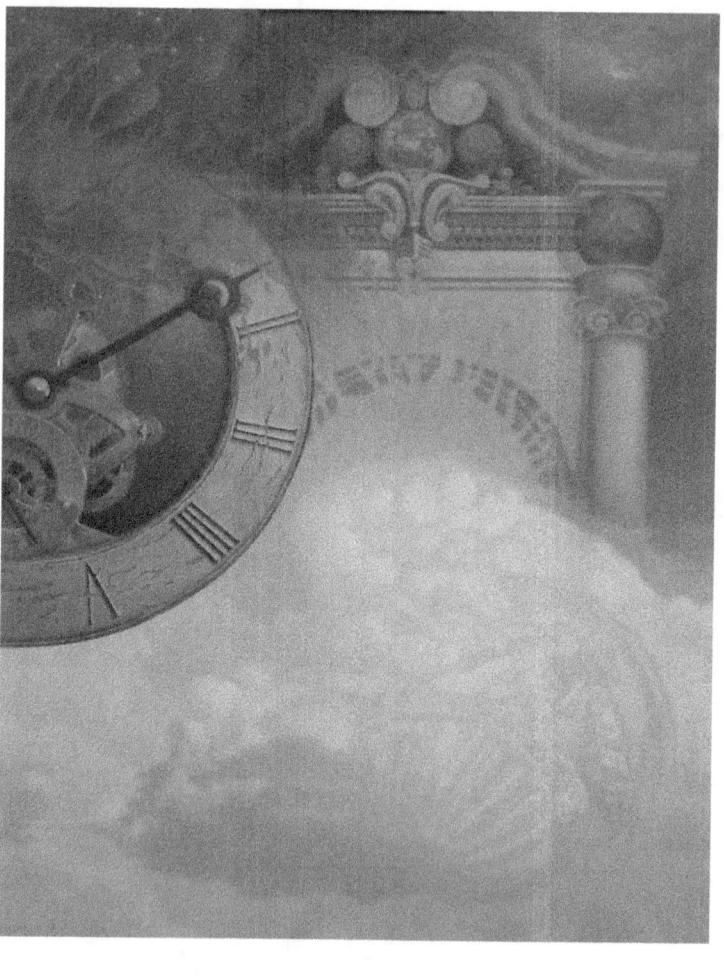

I need the quiet solitude,
of my painting studio.

I love the creative adventures;
we go on in the enchanted domains,
of our studios.

Right?

I also need the exciting world of exhibiting,
in the International Artistic' Extraordinaire!

I enjoy coming out into the global art scene,
we all hear about as we paint;

And paint...

   And paint...

     And paint...

But, I am going there;

Now!

Fame Game

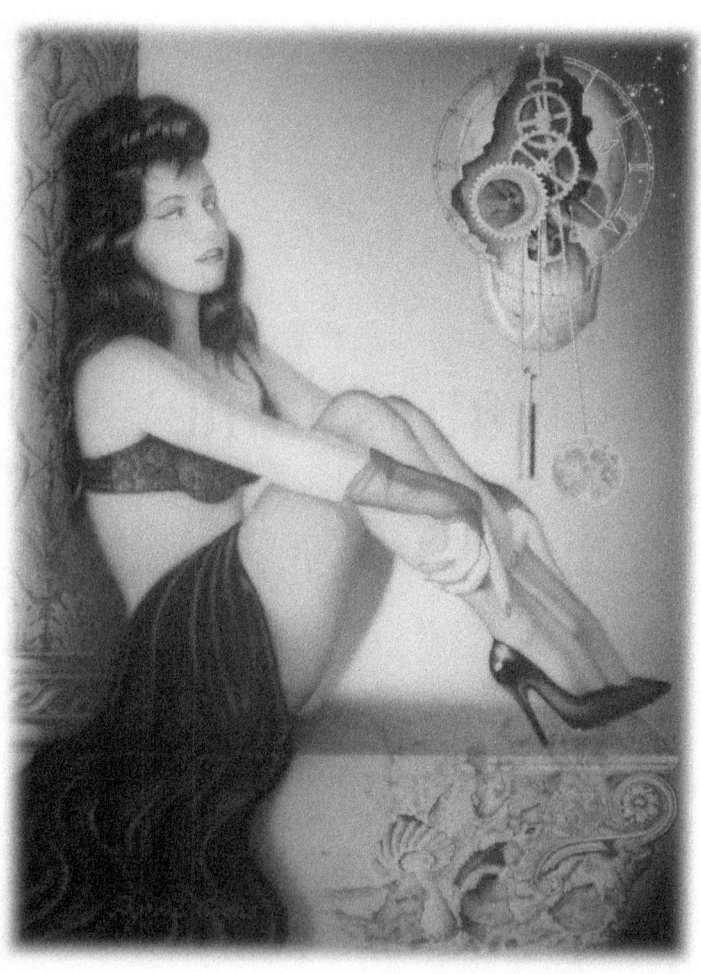

But how fond we become of ourselves,

how all-consuming our callings can be.

Bitch of sweet Fame,

so strong your addictive allure.

I have waited so patiently for *my* time in your shining light;

my turn to bask in the warm glow of your vanity and treasure.

To you I surrender.

Game over.

Moon over The Mission

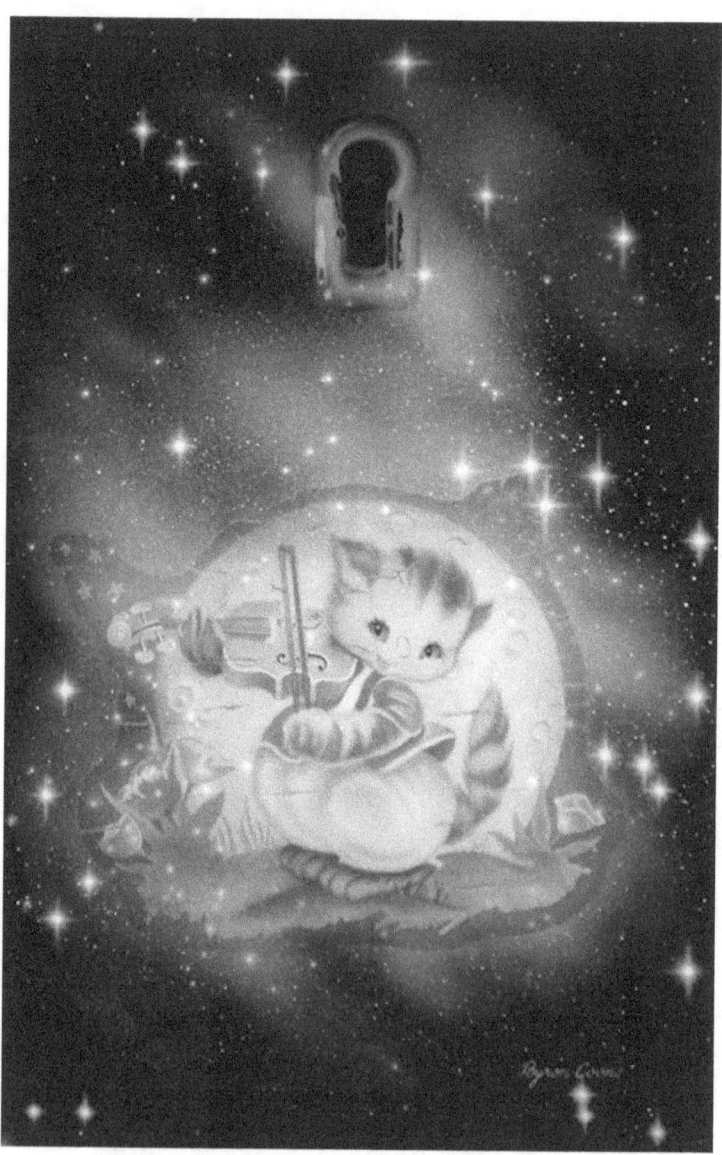

Hills upon hills of flickering street lights on invisible strings,

Line up twisting roads and narrow hidden alleyways.

First Quarter hovering high over the rolling city.

I have come to live here if only in my mind.

I am on my own like Snow White, lost;

in your haunted wood at night.

But feel a freedom like I have never known;

or, is this a feeling I had just forgotten?

Now, gratefully remembered.

WOW
Trans March 2012
San Francisco

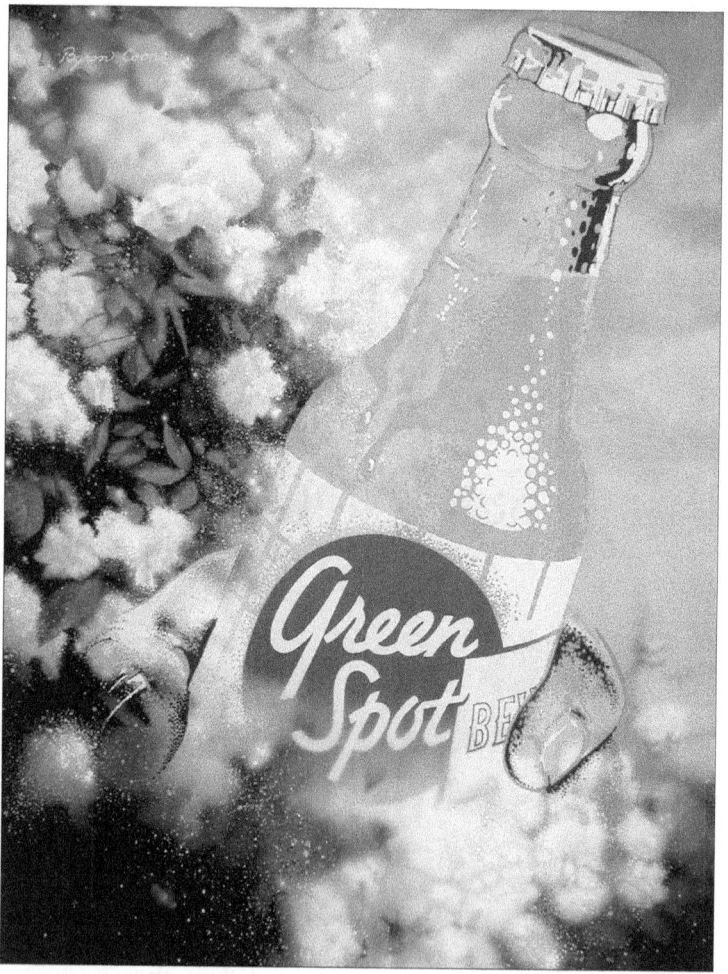

We rolled into the city by underground express

to emerge upon crowded streets; facing,

a bright green hillside covered by colorful people,

in a rainbow of gender identities.

How utterly incredible we all looked standing

in the warm summer sun; hoping,

with hard earned smiles of valor, liberation and love,

as if it were nineteen sixty-seven.

The Magical Metropolis stretched her hilly body out before us; willing,

I couldn't take enough pictures of everything and everybody,

prideful posturing and posing everywhere.

A day to Show-n-Tell our emotional eclectic stories; sharing,

our non-violent vendettas with strangers standing,

at the convivial Trans March[6] parade;

All...if only for ourselves.

---

[6] The San Francisco Trans March is one of the largest transgender Pride events in the entire world.

#newGirl

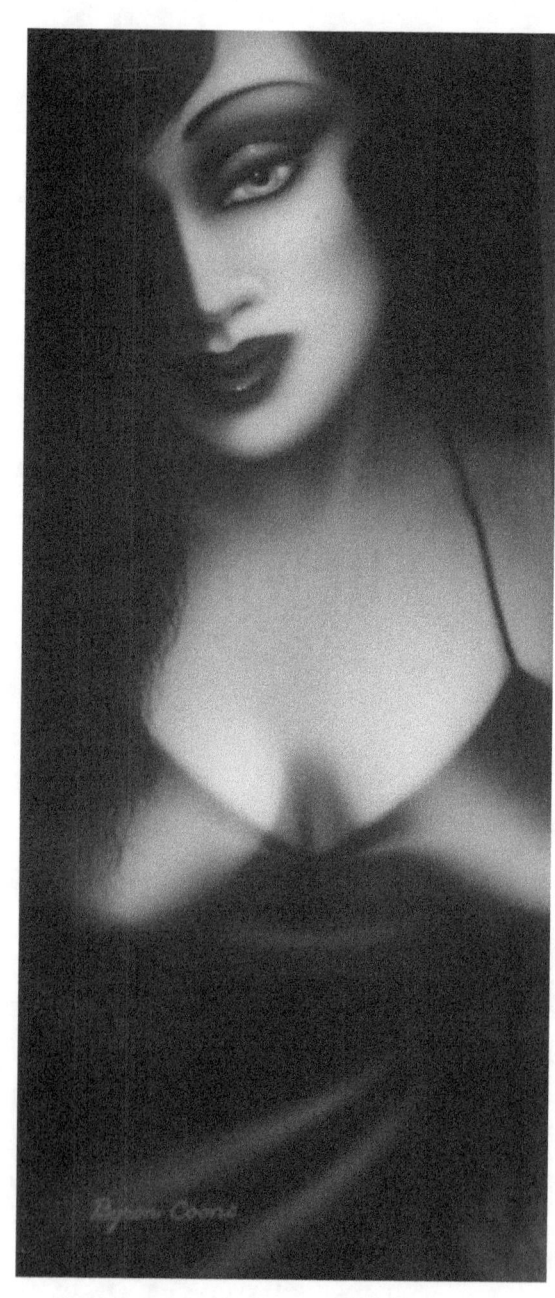

There's a new girl in town.

She isn't like the other girls.

You may have seen her around.

She doesn't follow all the rules.

The world has never seen,

a girl like this before.

She's knockin' on-the-door.

Let her in!

Let her out...

Let her be.

Beauty Bare

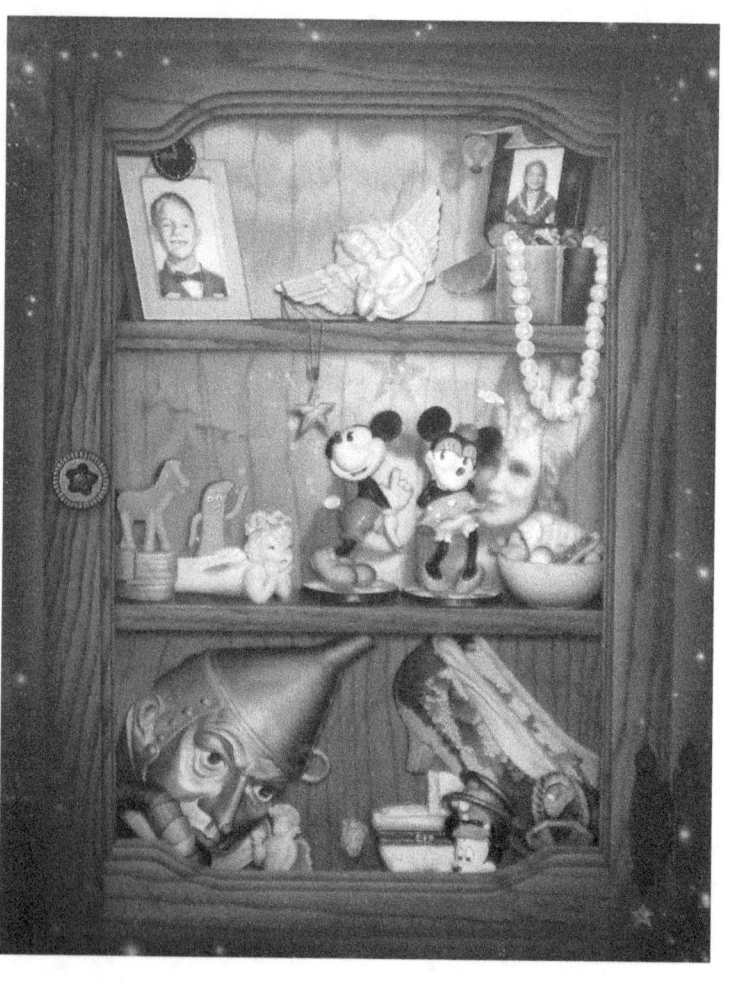

Beauty smiled quietly across to me.

Graciously, I returned her favor.

Edna you wrote it so true,

"Euclid alone has looked on beauty bare." [7]

You could have not expressed it more clearly to me,

and listen still to her massive sandal set on stone.

How beautiful your deep echoing words.

I risk a prattling poem with mine.

---

[7] One Who Might Have Become a Message by Edna St. Vincent Millay 1923

Millennia

Looking through the lucid blue-green glass of my mind,
I can see clearly through the endless equations of time.

And know by instinct;
My millennium has come at last.

Every moment,

Quiet thought,

Spoken word,

Soft breath...

Precious treasures.

I Was the Bookworm

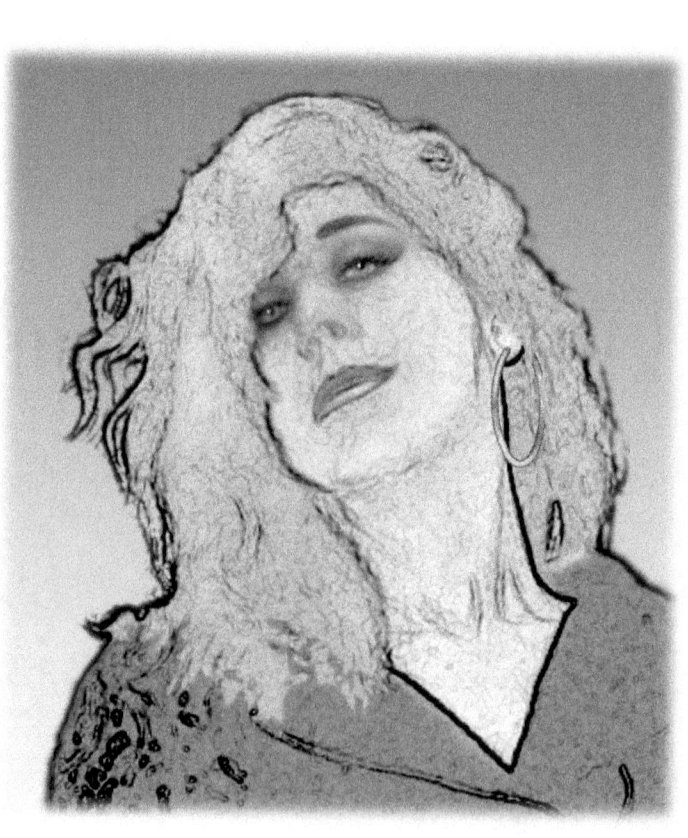

Softly hidden under my long brown hair,

behind gold wireframe tortoise shell glasses,

dreaming nestled deeply in my old green chair;

I was the bookworm.

Wonderfully lost in the pages

of someone else's thoughts and feelings,

castaway into the faraway chapters of their desires and dreams,

quietly secluded inside fortresses of fiction and fantasy;

I was the bookworm.

Momentarily,

I would come up to the surface of life,

only to silently retreat.

I was the bookworm...

No more.